CONTENTS

Copyright © MCMLXXX by

ASHLEY PUBLICATIONS, INC.
263 Veterans Blvd., Carlstadt, N.J. 07072

Cavatina.

JOACHIM RAFF. Op. 85 No 3.

Larghetto quasi Andantino. (♩ = 76)

Légende.

HENRI WIENIAWSKI. Op.17.

Barcarole.

L. SPOHR. Op.135.

Adagio from Violin Concerto № 8.

L. SPOHR. Op. 47.

Andante from Violin Concerto.

MENDELSSOHN. Op. 64.

29

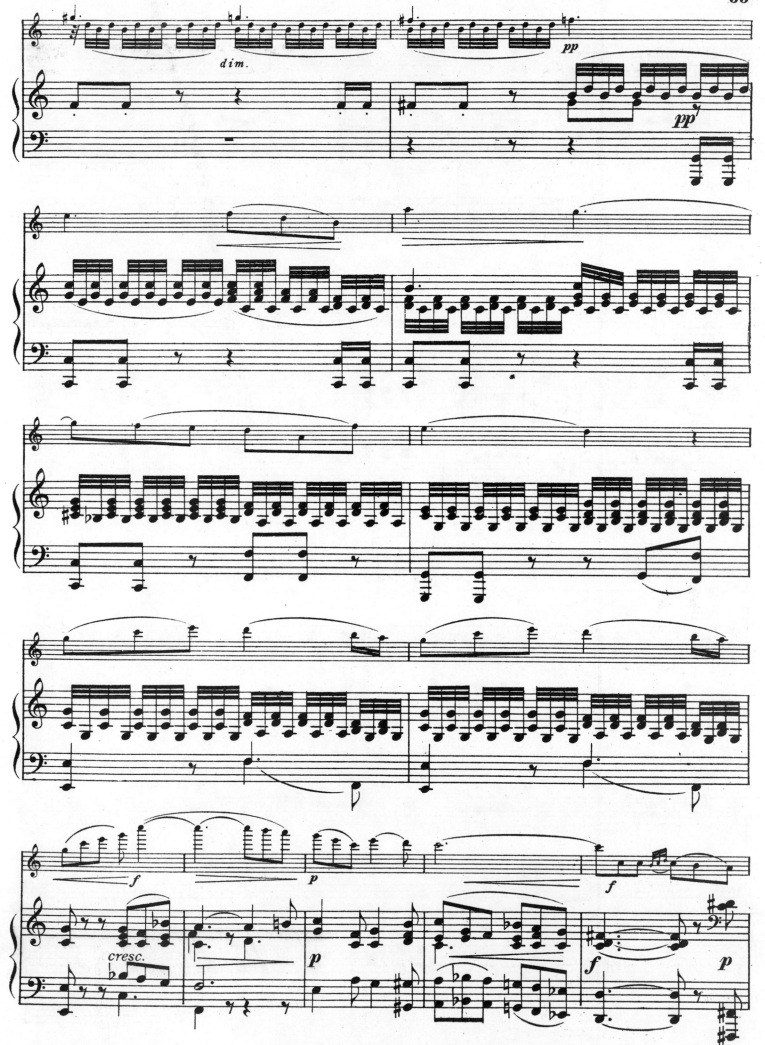

Adagio.

MOZART.

Romance in G.

L. v. BEETHOVEN. Op. 40.

Romance in F.

L.v. BEETHOVEN. Op.50.

Fantaisie
ou
SCÈNE DE BALLET

C. de BÉRIOT. Op. 100.

Allegro vivace.

Tempo di bolero.

Valse moderato.

poco rall.

colla parte.

a tempo

a tempo.

Allegro appassionato.

Chanson Polonaise.

H. WIENIAWSKI. Op. 12.

Méditation.

AVE MARIA.

Sur le Ier Prélude de J. S. Bach.

CHARLES GOUNOD.

Largo.

'Serse'

HANDEL.

Loure.

J. S. BACH.

Ballade.

BERNHARD MOLIQUE.

Andante espressivo.

poco agitato e cresc.

Adagio and Allegro from Sonata № 11.

CORELLI.

Allegro.

6me Air Varie.

C. de BÉRIOT. Op. 12.

INTRODUCTION.
Adagio.

Moderato.

1er VAR

Maestoso grandioso.

4me VAR.

Più lento.

con espress.

Air.

BERNHARD MOLIQUE.

Aria.

J. S. BACH.

Fantasia.

P. RODE. Op. 24.

Kuyawiak.

MAZURKA.

HENRY WIENIAWSKI.

Polonaise Brillante.

HENRY WIENIAWSKI.
Op. 4

Scherzino.

JOACHIM RAFF. Op. 84 No 4.

Air Varié.

P. RODE. Op. 16.

Adagio.

Andante un poco allegretto.

VAR. 1.

Un poco più di molto.

con forza.

Rêverie.

HENRY VIEUXTEMPS. Op. 22. Nº 3.

Air Varié.

P. RODE. Op.10.

VAR. III.

Un poco Adagio.

VAR. IV.

Tempo primo.

Engraved & Printed by "The Soho Press" London.